WORLD OF
DISCOVERY

TITANIC

All you ever wanted to know!

TITANIC

igloobooks

igl00books

Published in 2012
by Igloo Books Ltd
Cottage Farm
Sywell
NN6 0BJ

www.igloobooks.com

OCE001 0912

2 4 6 8 10 9 7 5 3

ISBN: 978-0-85780-777-9

Printed and manufactured in China

Written by Brian Williams

Contents

What was *Titanic*?

When people hear the name *"Titanic"*, they think of a ship that sank. Many stories surround this great ship that made just one fatal voyage across the Atlantic.

In the early 1900s, airplanes were small and slow, and no airplane had yet flown across a vast ocean. Instead, ocean liners carried hundreds of people on regular routes across the oceans. *Titanic* was built to carry about 2,500 passengers across the Atlantic from Europe to the United Sates in about five days. It was the biggest ship in the world in 1912. No ship this big had ever left a shipyard or steamed into any port. At her launch, *Titanic* was the pride of the seas.

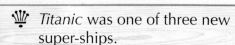

FASCINATING FACTS

- *Titanic* was one of three new super-ships.

- The other two ships were *Olympic* and *Gigantic* (later renamed *Britannic*).

- All three ships were owned by the British shipping company called the White Star Line.

The giant Atlas, who carried the world on his shoulders, was one of the 12 Titans or super-gods of ancient Greece and Rome. The word "titanic" came to mean anything gigantic.

Data Diary

- In 1845 the White Star Line shipping company is started in Liverpool, England. It operates traditional sailing vessels, called clippers, mainly to Australia. Their most important cargo is gold.

- In 1867 the White Star Line goes bankrupt and is bought by Thomas Henry Ismay. The company teams up with Belfast shipbuilders Harland and Wolff. Their first liner is *Oceanic*, launched in 1870.

A poster advertises the White Star Line's new super-ship *Titanic*. No ship so big or so luxurious had ever put to sea before.

In April 1912, *Titanic* set out on its first crossing of the North Atlantic Ocean. More than halfway across, the ship hit an iceberg and sank. More than 1,500 people drowned. This very sad story is why so many people still remember the *Titanic*.

Did you know

- Traditionally, ships were always referred to as "she".

- Two or more ships of the same class, or built to virtually the same design, were known as "sister ships".

- Modern sister ships include the Royal Caribbean International's *Explorer of the Seas* and *Adventure of the Seas*.

Crossing the oceans

Until the 1830s, the only way to cross an ocean was by sailing ship. Big sailing ships carried migrants and gold-seekers from Europe to America. They carried cargo, too, such as tea from China and wool from Australia. Then steamships began to take over.

Most early steamships had sails as well as steam engines and paddle wheels. This meant they could still sail if they ran out of coal. Before long, steamships began to take over from sailing ships. Unlike sailing ships, they could travel at a constant speed on fixed schedules following specific routes. Gradually, bigger and faster steamships were built.

Ships' passengers packed their belongings in sturdy "cabin trunks". Trunks were strong enough to stand being thrown about by dock-workers or rough seas!

Did you know

- One of the first American transatlantic steamers was the sidewheel steamer SS *Hermann,* built in 1847 in New York City.

- The SS *Hermann* at first carried just 188 passengers (later increased to 340). It sailed between New York and Germany via Southampton in England.

This White Star Line postcard, sent from *Titanic* on 11th April, 1912, shows *Titanic* dwarfing a much smaller sailing ship.

Data Diary

- In 1819 the SS *Savannah*, part sailing ship and part sidewheel steamer, becomes the first steamship to cross the Atlantic Ocean – although it mostly uses sail.

- The first ship to cross the Atlantic using just steam power is the SS *Sirius* in 1838. This sidewheel steamship was built to sail between London and Cork in Ireland.

- The SS *Sirius* was racing to beat Isambard Kingdom Brunel's SS *Great Western*. *Sirius* set off four days earlier, and had to burn cabin furniture and a mast after its coal ran low. It beat the *Great Western* by just one day!

By 1900, fast ocean liners were steaming across the Atlantic in less than a week. The busiest route was between Europe and the United States. People went for business and pleasure aboard fast, floating luxury hotels.

World's biggest ship

Before *Titanic*, the world's biggest ship was an iron sailing steam ship – the *Great Eastern*.

Designed by Isambard Kingdom Brunel, it was launched in 1858. Brunel's ship was five times bigger than any ship before it (it was 18,915 tons). It could carry 4,000 passengers and 418 crew. However, it was not a great success because it rolled in the water, scaring the passengers, and its steam engines were too small. It was broken up for scrap in 1889. In 1906 the shipping line Cunard launched its ocean giant *Mauretania*. It was 33,000 tons and had four turbine engines driving four propellers.

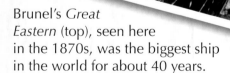

Data Diary

⚓ In 1899 Joseph Bruce Ismay succeeds his father as head of the White Star Line.

⚓ In 1907 Ismay and William Pirrie, head of Harland and Wolff shipbuilders, discuss plans to build two new ocean liners to rival Cunard's ships in luxury.

⚓ On 29th July, 1908, White Star approves Harland and Wolff's designs for the two new liners, *Olympic* and *Titanic*.

Brunel's *Great Eastern* (top), seen here in the 1870s, was the biggest ship in the world for about 40 years.

When *Titanic* (above) was built, it became the world's biggest ship. Here it can be seen towering over people on the dockside.

Did you know

- *Great Eastern* was first named *Leviathan* (after a sea monster).

- *Great Eastern* was the only ship to have a propeller, paddle wheels and sails.

- Cunard's *Mauretania* was the fastest Atlantic ship for 20 years, until 1929.

Mauretania and its sister ship *Lusitania* became the new, fast "queens of the seas". Each could carry over 2,000 passengers and 800 crew, and could steam across the Atlantic in just four to five days. Cunard's rival on the Atlantic route was the White Star Line. In 1907 White Star ordered two new giant ships. One of them, *Titanic*, was to be the biggest ship in the world!

The elegant First Class dining room on Cunard's *Lusitania* attracted some very rich passengers.

FASCINATING FACTS

- The big liners were able to charge high prices to First Class passengers, who had the best cabins and best food.

- A First Class ticket cost roughly 30 times more than a Third Class ticket.

- *Mauretania* could carry 563 passengers in First Class, 464 in Second Class and 1,138 in Third Class.

1908 Sea giants

White Star wanted its new ships to be the absolute height of luxury, comfort and style. While Cunard's ships were built to be fast, White Star's fleet would be the biggest and most luxurious ships.

White Star's boss, Joseph Bruce Ismay, chose the Belfast shipyard of Harland and Wolff to build his ships. Its chief, Lord William Pirrie, agreed to supply White Star with two giant liners. The ships were going to be so huge that the shipyard had to build two new slipways for them. Above these was a massive gantry (like a bridge), used to swing the heavy steel plates into place.

Data Diary

✿ On 31st July, 1908, White Star and Harland and Wolff sign a contract agreeing to build *Olympic* and *Titanic*, with a third sister ship, *Britannic*, to follow.

✿ In December 1908, building work starts – *Olympic*'s keel is laid. The keel is the long piece of metal at the bottom of a ship's hull, or body.

The White Star Line printed a brochure comparing the size of *Titanic* and *Olympic* with the tallest skyscrapers in New York City.

Did you know ?

- "Starboard" is the right side of a ship (as seen from on board facing front).
- "Port" is the left side of a ship (as seen from on board facing front).
- The front of a ship is the "bow" and the rear end is the "stern".

Titanic (on the right) was almost identical to its sister ship *Olympic*.

Titanic's chief designer was Thomas Andrews (William Pirrie's nephew). Born in Ireland in 1873, he started work in the shipyard at the age of 16. Andrews and his team planned every part of the ship, from the rudder and propellers to the bathrooms in the First Class cabins. As the plans took shape, everyone was amazed by the size of the two massive new ships.

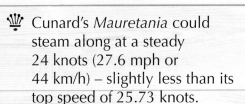

FASCINATING FACTS

- Cunard's *Mauretania* could steam along at a steady 24 knots (27.6 mph or 44 km/h) – slightly less than its top speed of 25.73 knots.
- 1 knot = 1 nautical (sea) mile an hour. A nautical mile is slightly longer than a land mile.
- Ismay hoped that *Titanic* would be as fast as *Mauretania*.

Titanic takes shape

1909

Titanic was built in stages. The shipbuilders' first job was to lay the keel. This was the "backbone" of the ship.

Metal ribs were then attached to the keel to make a frame, which was like a skeleton. Steel plates were attached to the ribs and fixed in place with metal pegs, called rivets. The rivets were hammered in place through holes drilled in the metal, and then beaten flat to stop them falling out.

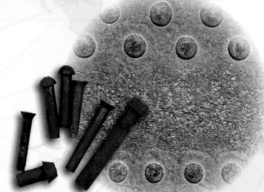

This close-up of a ship's steel plate shows the flattened heads of the rivets that attached the overlapping plates together.

Did you know

- Harland and Wolff are still in business in Belfast today, making offshore drilling rigs and wind-farm platforms, as well as ships.

Titanic takes shape in Belfast. The hull's metal plates are clearly visible, and the ship's name can be seen high on the bow.

Data Diary

- On 31st March, 1909, *Titanic's* keel is laid.
- *By April 1910, the massive steel frame is ready to have the steel plates attached.*
- On 19th October, 1910, the last of the ship's steel plates are riveted into place. The metal plates form a "skin" 25 mm (1 in.) thick.
- On 20th October, 1910, *Olympic's* hull is launched into the water.

FASCINATING FACTS

- *Titanic* was given shipyard number 401 and it was built on Slipway 3.
- Over 3 million rivets were hammered into *Titanic's* hull.
- Some riveters developed hearing problems because their hammering made so much noise.
- Unlike *Titanic*, many big ships today are put together in factory-made sections. The sections are joined together to make the hull.

Launch day

MAY 31ST 1911

It took the skilled Irish shipbuilders at Harland and Wolff two years to finish *Titanic*'s hull. Once complete, it was time to launch the ship, even though it was still just an empty shell.

Thousands of people cheered and waved as *Titanic* slid into the water for the first time.

The launch date was set for 31st May, 1911. In Belfast, 100,000 people crowded into the Harland and Wolff shipyard to watch the great event.

As soon as the wedges holding the ship were knocked away and the heavy chains let go, the huge ship slid down the slipway into the water for the first time. The crowd cheered and men waved their caps. The bosses of the White Star Line and Harland and Wolff celebrated the great day, and a big lunch was held for important visitors at Belfast's Grand Central Hotel.

Launch

OF

White Star Royal Mail Triple-Screw Steamer

"TITANIC"

At BELFAST,

Wednesday, 31st May, 1911, at 12·15 p.m.

Admit Bearer.

Tickets for the *Titanic* launch showed the White Star Line's trademark red flag with a white star.

FASCINATING FACTS

- *Titanic* took just 62 seconds to slide down the slipway.

- The huge, heavy ship moved so quickly because the slipway had been greased with 22 tons of tallow (animal fat) and soap.

Once launched, there was still a great deal of work to be done to make *Titanic* ready for its first passengers.

Did you know

- Launches could be dangerous events. At *Titanic*'s launch, one unfortunate worker was struck by a piece of wood on the slipway. He was rushed to hospital, but died the next day.

- Thomas Andrews' nephew John (aged 5) helped to knock out one of the wedges holding the ship.

After its launch, *Titanic* was towed to the fitting-out wharf, where it took almost a year to install the ship's engines, boilers, funnels, rooms and navigating equipment.

Data Diary

- On 31st May, 1911, *Titanic* is launched at 12.13 pm.

- This date is also the birthday of Lord Pirrie (Harland and Wolff's boss) and his wife!

- Also on this day, *Titanic*'s sister-ship *Olympic* finishes its sea trials and is declared seaworthy.

The engines

1911

The empty shell of *Titanic* now had to be fitted out with massive boilers and engines. The engines burned coal to heat water into steam.

The owners of the White Star Line wanted *Titanic* to be able to sail as fast as Cunard's new ship, *Mauretania*. Its rival had four steam turbine engines driving four propellers. Turbine engines were still quite new in 1912. *Titanic*'s two huge engines were more old-fashioned. They were "reciprocating" engines, with moving parts that went up and down inside. There was also one smaller turbine engine. Each engine drove a massive propeller.

These are some of the massive boilers used by *Titanic*'s sister ship *Olympic*. They tower over the man half way along the gap.

Did you know

- *Titanic* had 160 stokers, or firemen, who shovelled coal into the furnaces day and night.

- Three of *Titanic*'s funnels puffed out gas and smoke from the engines. The fourth funnel was for show, put up to make the ship look more impressive! It was also used for storage and ventilation, to let fresh air in and stale air out.

Titanic's stokers sweated in heat and dust as they fed the boiler-furnaces with coal. They used shovels, barrows and lots of muscle power.

- *Titanic* had 159 furnaces, in which coal was burned to heat the water in the boilers.

- The ship had 29 metal boilers. The boilers were metal tanks with tubes inside full of water. Each boiler held over 48 tons of water.

- *Titanic's* three engines had the power of about 50,000 horses!

- The engines were 10 m (30 ft) tall – higher than five men.

Data Diary

- In May 1911, *Titanic's* engines are still in the shipyard's Engine Work's Erecting Shop. Over the next few months they are taken apart and moved, piece by piece, to the fitting-out wharf, where they are installed in *Titanic's* engine room.

Steam from *Titanic's* boilers was piped at high pressure into the engines' cylinders. The steam passed from one cylinder to the next, and was cleverly reused. Finally it was cooled back to water and the process started again. The engines were designed to give *Titanic* a speed of about 24 knots.

1911 Inside *Titanic*

At the fitting-out wharf, *Titanic*'s empty hull was transformed.

At the bottom of the ship, engineers installed the three great engines, 29 massive boilers and 159 furnaces, where the coal was burned. There were also six cargo holds for goods needing to be transported to America and for luggage not needed on the trip. The lower decks also contained the coal bunkers (big enough to carry 8,000 tons of coal), a squash court, a mail room, food freezers, crew rooms and some of the Third Class sleeping quarters. There was also a Turkish bath and swimming pool for First Class passengers, and a Third Class dining saloon.

FASCINATING FACTS

- About 3,000 workers were employed to build *Titanic*.

- *Titanic* measured 269 m (882 ft 9 in.) long – just 10 cm (4 in.) longer than *Olympic*!

- *Titanic*'s width (or "beam") was 28 m (92 ft) and it was 53 m (175 ft) high from the keel to the funnel tops.

The ship was fitted out with all kinds of beautiful furniture, including this Chippendale-style wooden chair.

Second Class cabins were on the upper, middle and lower decks. D deck was fitted out with a huge reception room and dining saloon for First Class passengers. Two Grand Staircases led to the upper decks, where some of the First Class cabins were found, along with a restaurant, a Parisian-style café and smoking rooms for the men.

Data Diary

- Throughout 1911, *Titanic*'s empty hull is turned into a floating palace.

- In July 1911, J. Bruce Ismay announces that *Titanic*'s maiden (first) voyage will depart on 20th March, 1912 (later moved to 10th April).

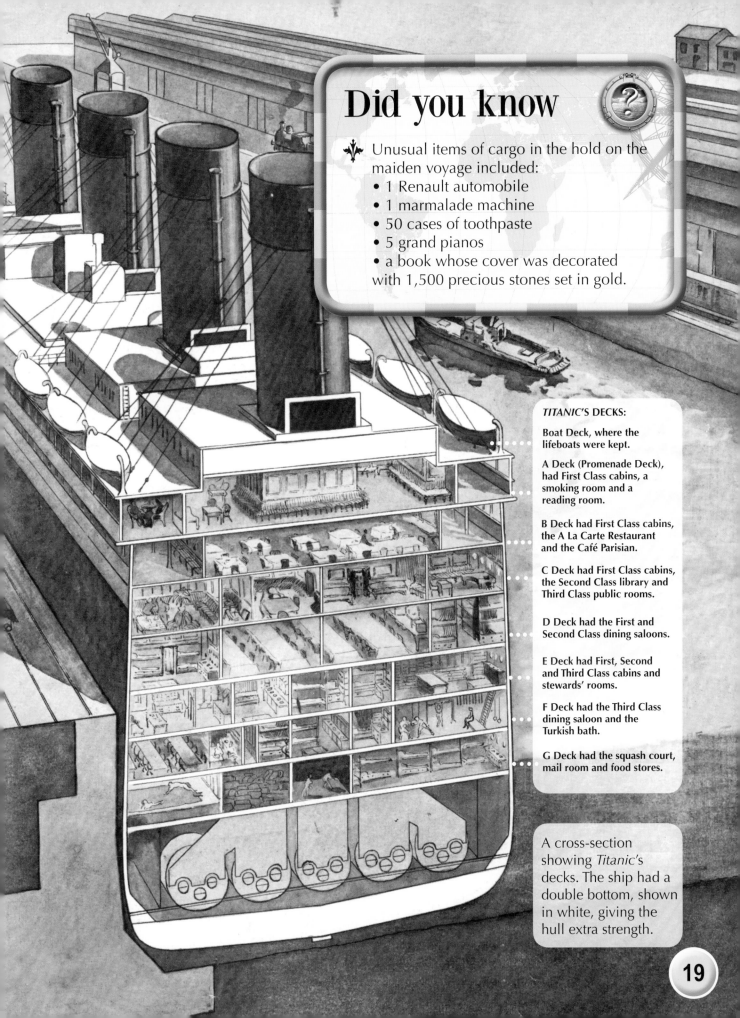

Did you know

- Unusual items of cargo in the hold on the maiden voyage included:
  - 1 Renault automobile
  - 1 marmalade machine
  - 50 cases of toothpaste
  - 5 grand pianos
  - a book whose cover was decorated with 1,500 precious stones set in gold.

TITANIC'S DECKS:

Boat Deck, where the lifeboats were kept.

A Deck (Promenade Deck), had First Class cabins, a smoking room and a reading room.

B Deck had First Class cabins, the A La Carte Restaurant and the Café Parisian.

C Deck had First Class cabins, the Second Class library and Third Class public rooms.

D Deck had the First and Second Class dining saloons.

E Deck had First, Second and Third Class cabins and stewards' rooms.

F Deck had the Third Class dining saloon and the Turkish bath.

G Deck had the squash court, mail room and food stores.

A cross-section showing *Titanic*'s decks. The ship had a double bottom, shown in white, giving the hull extra strength.

19

1911

Getting ready for sea

Workers swarmed all over *Titanic*, turning it into a magnificent hotel.

The ship's funnels were installed, and the funnels and hull were painted. The five anchors arrived, each so heavy that 20 horses were needed to pull them! The massive rudder, weighing 100 tons, was also fitted. At sea, the rudder had its own steam engine to move it from side to side when a change of course was needed.

Titanic's rudder and propeller shaft are fitted by Belfast shipyard workers. They can be seen here dwarfed by the massive machinery.

Did you know

- The ship's official name was RMS *Titanic*. RMS stands for Royal Mail Steamer.

- One of *Titanic*'s jobs was to carry mail between Britain and the United States.

- *Titanic* had a mail room, where mail clerks would sort letters and parcels.

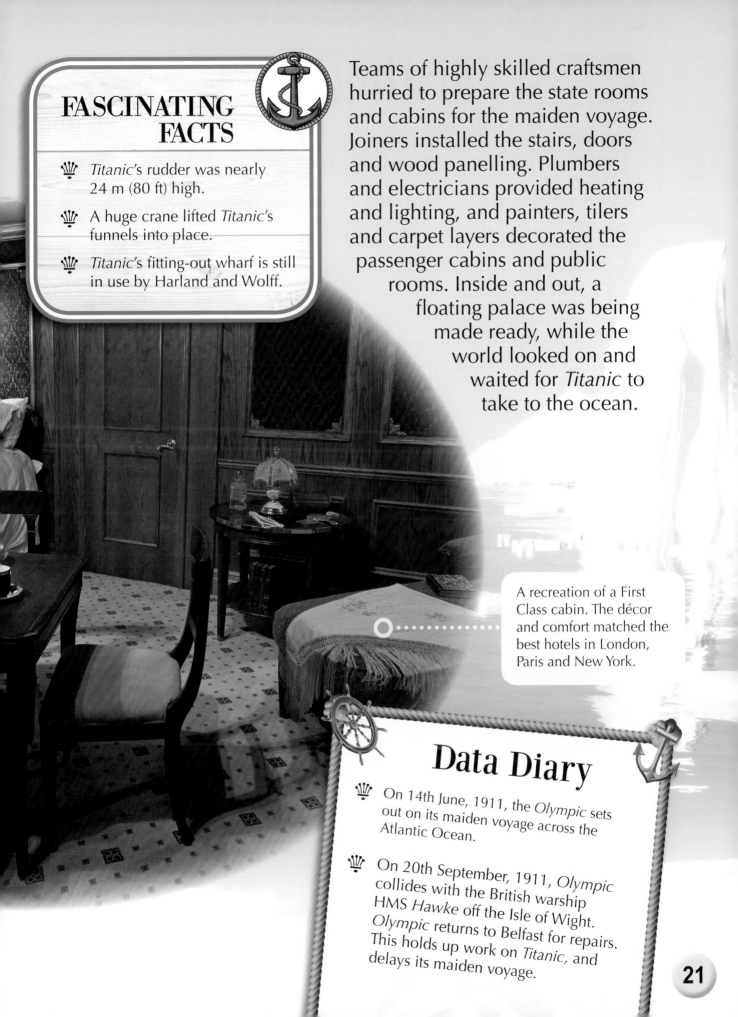

- *Titanic's* rudder was nearly 24 m (80 ft) high.

- A huge crane lifted *Titanic's* funnels into place.

- *Titanic's* fitting-out wharf is still in use by Harland and Wolff.

Teams of highly skilled craftsmen hurried to prepare the state rooms and cabins for the maiden voyage. Joiners installed the stairs, doors and wood panelling. Plumbers and electricians provided heating and lighting, and painters, tilers and carpet layers decorated the passenger cabins and public rooms. Inside and out, a floating palace was being made ready, while the world looked on and waited for *Titanic* to take to the ocean.

A recreation of a First Class cabin. The décor and comfort matched the best hotels in London, Paris and New York.

Data Diary

- On 14th June, 1911, the *Olympic* sets out on its maiden voyage across the Atlantic Ocean.

- On 20th September, 1911, *Olympic* collides with the British warship HMS *Hawke* off the Isle of Wight. *Olympic* returns to Belfast for repairs. This holds up work on *Titanic,* and delays its maiden voyage.

1912 A floating hotel

The *Illustrated London Ne[w]*
featured pictures of *Titan[ic]*
luxurious rooms, includi[ng]
a First Class cabin with fo[ur]
poster bed (centre right), [the]
pool (bottom left) and the C[afé]
Parisian (top le[ft])

By the time the fitting out was complete, *Titanic* had everything its passengers could want or need!

The Parisian-style café had big windows so that diners could look out to sea. This was a new feature on a British ship. The main dining saloon for First Class passengers was decorated in Jacobean style and could seat up to 500 people. Alternatively, they could eat in the À la Carte Restaurant, sometimes referred to as "the Ritz", after the famous London hotel. The aim was for people on board to forget they were on a ship and imagine themselves in a city hotel or grand country house.

Data Diary

 On 25th March, 1912, the ship's lifeboats are tested.

 On 31st March, 1912, *Titanic*'s fitting out is completed.

 By 1st April, 1912, only the finishing touches remain to be done to the ship.

Titanic's gymnasium included cycles, a rowing machine and even an electric camel!

There was a telephone system for passengers, a library and hairdressers. After exercising in the pool or gymnasium, or on the squash court, First Class passengers could relax in hot tubs and steam rooms, or in the "electric bath". Even the Third Class public rooms were above standard, with smart wooden panels and comfortable chairs.

FASCINATING FACTS

- Cabins for First Class passengers had private baths.
- Third Class cabins slept between 2 and 10 people.
- The "electric bath" was an early type of tanning bed.

Titanic's First Class passengers used the glass-domed Grand Staircase (this is a re-creation) to move between the Boat Deck and cabins on E Deck.

Did you know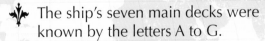

- The ship's seven main decks were known by the letters A to G.
- The portholes on G Deck (the lowest passenger deck) were only just above the waterline.

Sea trials

Before any ship starts its working life, it must be tested at sea to make sure everything works. *Titanic* did its sea trials on 2nd April, 1912.

Data Diary

☙ On 2nd April, *Titanic* undergoes one day of sea trials, then returns to Belfast. It leaves Belfast at 8.00 pm for Southampton, its new home port. Although registered at the port of Liverpool, *Titanic* never visited the city.

☙ On 3rd April, 1912, *Titanic* docks in Southampton, ready to start loading.

In Southampton, everything was made ready for *Titanic*'s first transatlantic voyage.

The sea trials were *Titanic*'s first test in the open sea. As the ship steamed out of Belfast, engineers checked how the engines behaved and made sure the rudder and propellers were just right. *Titanic*'s sister ship *Olympic* was already busy crossing the Atlantic Ocean.

Titanic at sea was a spectacular sight. This shot from the 1997 *Titanic* movie shows the ship at speed.

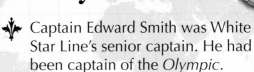
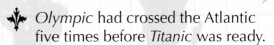
On the evening of April 2nd, a small "skeleton" crew, including chief designer Thomas Andrews, took *Titanic* on its first voyage. The new captain, Edward Smith, was not yet on board. *Titanic* steamed from Ireland around the west coast of Britain, then east up the English Channel to Southampton, where it arrived on 3rd April.

FASCINATING FACTS

- At sea, *Titanic* became the biggest man-made moving object ever (at that time).

- Its gross tonnage (the weight of a passenger ship) was 46,328 tons.

APRIL 1912

Captain and crew

In Southampton, the sea trials team finished any last-minute checks and left the ship, and *Titanic*'s crew came aboard.

In command of everyone on board was the captain. He felt proud to be in charge of the biggest ship in the world. Working with him were his officers and crew (about 885 people). Most of the crew had been hired in March and now saw the ship for the first time. They would run the ship and look after its passengers. Many came from the Southampton area.

FASCINATING FACTS

- The five postal clerks on board worked for the UK Royal Mail and US Postal Service.

- The radio operators worked for the Marconi Company.

- The deck crew included able bodied seamen, lamp trimmers, lookouts, surgeons, storekeepers and window cleaners, among others.

Captain Edward Smith had made the transatlantic route to New York many times.

Among the crew were the engineers and stokers, who looked after the engines and furnaces. There were also bakers, butchers, cooks, porters and pantrymen. Other crew served meals, tidied cabins, washed and cleaned, and looked after the gymnasium.

Data Diary

♕ By 6th April, 1912, all the crew positions on *Titanic* have been filled. Coal and the cargo for New York is loaded aboard.

♕ On 8th April, 1912, fresh food is loaded from the dockside and stored on board.

♕ On 10th April, 1912, Captain Smith goes aboard *Titanic* and takes command.

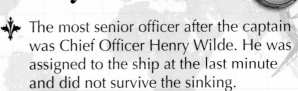

A maid-servant packs a few belongings before taking up her new job as one of the crew. *Titanic* had 23 women crew members, mostly stewardesses.

A butler polishes the silver. *Titanic's* "victualling" staff did similar work, though some rich passengers took their own butlers.

The ship had its own band of eight musicians. There was also a printer, who made a daily newspaper, passing on world news from the ship's radio operators.

Did you know

❦ The most senior officer after the captain was Chief Officer Henry Wilde. He was assigned to the ship at the last minute and did not survive the sinking.

❦ Violet Constance Jessop was one of *Titanic's* First Class stewardesses. She was aboard *Olympic* when it collided with HMS *Hawke*, aboard *Titanic* when it struck the iceberg, and aboard *Britannic* when it hit a mine!

APRIL 10TH 1912

Who was who?

Newspapers printed lists of the rich and famous passengers on Atlantic crossings, so everyone knew who was who on *Titanic*'s first voyage.

Among the liner's First Class passengers was one of the world's wealthiest men – John Jacob Astor IV. He booked to join *Titanic* at Cherbourg in France, the first stop after Southampton. Astor was taking his new young wife, Madeleine, back to the United States after a holiday in Egypt. She was expecting a baby. With them went three servants.

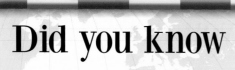

J. J. Astor was a writer, inventor and multi-millionaire.

Did you know

- Millionaire J. P. Morgan decided at the last minute not to sail on the *Titanic*.

- The exact number of people aboard is not known, but there were about 324 First Class passengers, about 277 in Second Class and about 708 in Third Class.

- *Titanic* was not full. It had room for over 1,000 First Class passengers, 510 in Second Class and more than 1,000 in Third Class.

London fashion designer Lady Lucy Duff-Gordon was on board with her husband Sir Cosmo, a wealthy landowner and fencing champion.

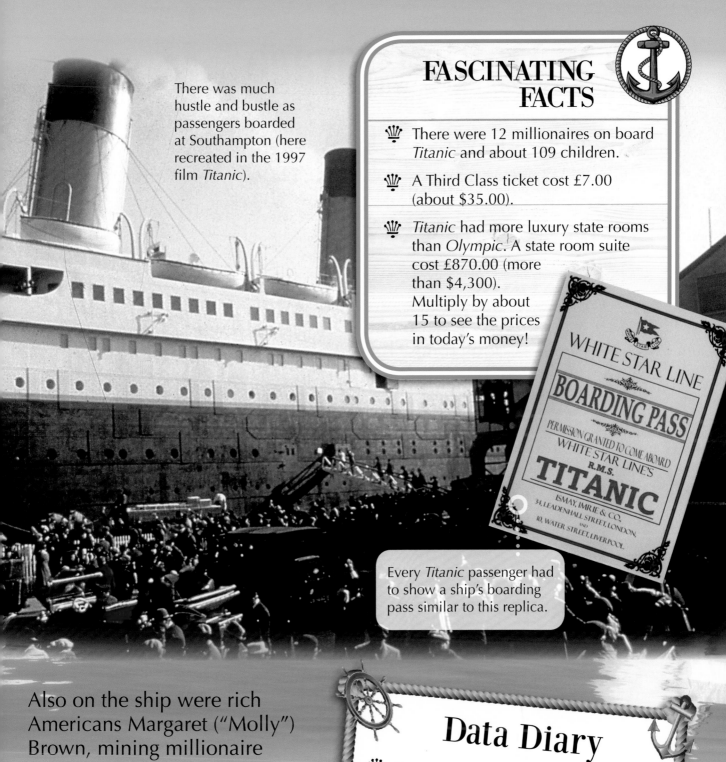

There was much hustle and bustle as passengers boarded at Southampton (here recreated in the 1997 film *Titanic*).

WHITE STAR LINE
BOARDING PASS
PERMISSION GRANTED TO COME ABOARD
WHITE STAR LINE'S
R.M.S.
TITANIC
ISMAY, IMRIE & CO.,
34, LEADENHALL STREET, LONDON,
AND
10, WATER STREET, LIVERPOOL.

Every *Titanic* passenger had to show a ship's boarding pass similar to this replica.

Also on the ship were rich Americans Margaret ("Molly") Brown, mining millionaire Benjamin Guggenheim and Isidor Straus (owner of Macy's department store in New York) with his wife Ida. Silent film star Dorothy Gibson was there too, along with White Star's J. Bruce Ismay and the ship's designer Thomas Andrews.

Data Diary

- Wednesday 10th April, 1912, is sailing day.

- Between 9.30 am and 11.30 am, the Second and Third Class boat trains arrive at the dockside. The passengers start to board and find their berths (sleeping places).

- At 11.30 am, the First Class boat train from London arrives. The passengers are escorted to their cabins.

APRIL 10TH 1912

Maiden voyage

At noon on 10th April, tug boats towed *Titanic* slowly out to sea. Everyone was excited – they were on their way to New York!

Getting out of port wasn't easy, however. As *Titanic* passed a smaller ship called the *New York*, *Titanic*'s wash broke all six of *New York*'s mooring ropes. The two ships almost collided, but a tug helped to keep the *New York* clear. Captain Smith ordered full power. After brief stops to pick up passengers at Cherbourg in France and Queenstown (now Cobh) in Ireland, *Titanic* headed west across the Atlantic Ocean. It was due to arrive in New York five days later.

FASCINATING FACTS

- US student tennis star Richard Williams joined the ship at Cherbourg with his father. He was pleased to find there was a squash court on board.

- Father Francis Brown left *Titanic* at Queenstown and took a last photograph of the ship leaving.

- Some 125 Irish migrants boarded at Queenstown – 14 of them from one village called Addergoole.

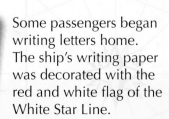

Some passengers began writing letters home. The ship's writing paper was decorated with the red and white flag of the White Star Line.

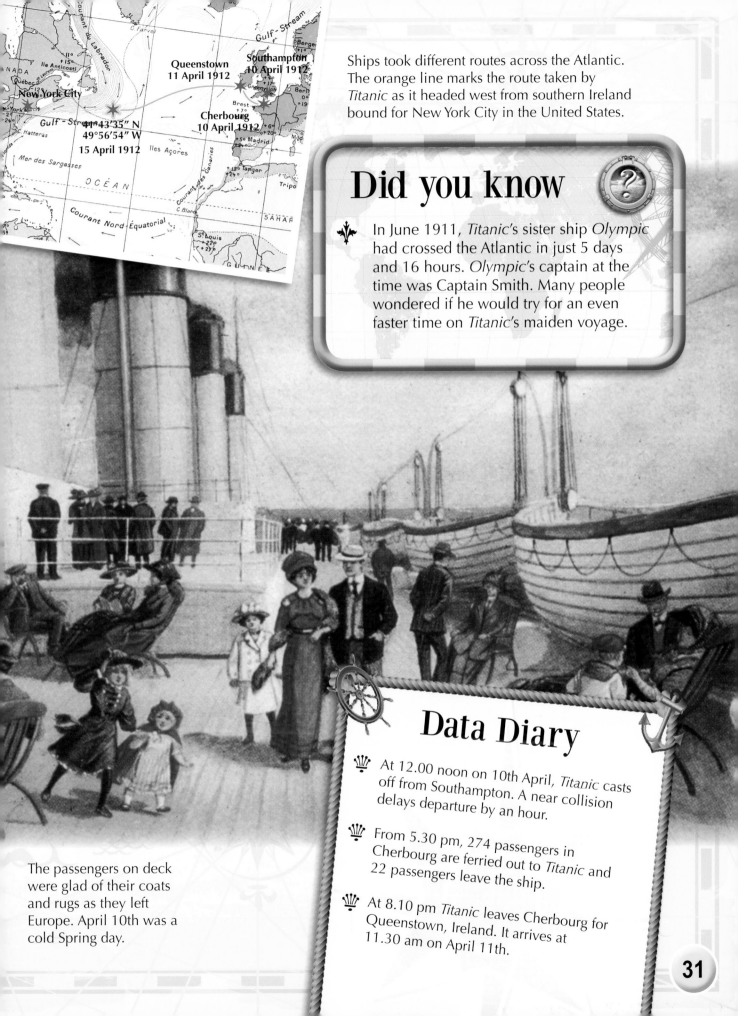

Ships took different routes across the Atlantic. The orange line marks the route taken by *Titanic* as it headed west from southern Ireland bound for New York City in the United States.

Did you know

- In June 1911, *Titanic*'s sister ship *Olympic* had crossed the Atlantic in just 5 days and 16 hours. *Olympic*'s captain at the time was Captain Smith. Many people wondered if he would try for an even faster time on *Titanic*'s maiden voyage.

The passengers on deck were glad of their coats and rugs as they left Europe. April 10th was a cold Spring day.

Data Diary

- At 12.00 noon on 10th April, *Titanic* casts off from Southampton. A near collision delays departure by an hour.

- From 5.30 pm, 274 passengers in Cherbourg are ferried out to *Titanic* and 22 passengers leave the ship.

- At 8.10 pm *Titanic* leaves Cherbourg for Queenstown, Ireland. It arrives at 11.30 am on April 11th.

New technology

Aboard the great ship, *Titanic's* passengers were able to enjoy all the latest gadgets of 1912, including electric lights and telephones.

Did you know

- *Titanic* was one of the first ships to be fitted out with wireless (radio), which was still a fairly new invention in 1912.

- The two wireless masts were 21 m (70 ft) tall, with wires slung between them.

- The ship's radio had a range of 1,600 km (1,000 mi.). It was installed mainly so rich passengers could send messages.

At night *Titanic* blazed with light made by its own electric generators.

Titanic's designer Thomas Andrews wanted the ship to be the last word in luxury, so an elaborate electricity supply was installed. Some 320 km (200 mi.) of electrical wires carried electricity all around the ship. Passengers in First Class could make a phone call to a friend in another cabin and then stroll down to try out one of the exercise bikes in the ship's gymnasium. Back home, electricity was still a fairly new idea outside of big cities. Many of the passengers' homes would have been lit by gaslight and oil lamps, or just candles.

FASCINATING FACTS

- ♕ Titanic had four generators and made enough electricity to light all the homes in a small city. The generators were near the stern.

- ♕ Electricity provided the power for the lighting, boat and engine room winches, cranes, watertight doors, elevators, heating and clocks.

- ♕ Titanic even had electric potato peelers, dough mixers and soup and sorbet makers!

The telegraphy office, or radio room, on Titanic provided state-of-the-art technology in 1912.

APRIL 12TH 1912

Upper and lower decks

Titanic's rich and poor passengers had rooms on different levels of the ship, and they did not mix.

The First Class cabins had feather beds, private baths and plenty of wardrobe space. Each class had its own promenade deck, where passengers could sit or stroll. On the First Class promenade deck, passengers near the bow were protected from sea spray by large sliding windows.

Fashionable ladies strolled through the First Class areas of the ship. One rich lady brought 17 trunks of clothes with her!

Did you know

- *Titanic* carried 20 lifeboats, enough for 1,178 people – although the ship had about 2,200 people on board when it sank and it was far from full.

- The lifeboats hung from small cranes, called davits, on the Boat Deck.

- Each of the 14 big lifeboats could hold 65 people. There were two small boats able to hold 40 people each and 4 collapsible (fold-up) boats that held 47 people each.

- At 1.30 pm on 11th April, 1912, *Titanic* raises its anchors and leaves Queenstown (now Cobh) in southern Ireland.

- On 12th and 13th April, *Titanic* sails through calm waters. Passengers stroll along 7 km (4.5 mi.) of deck by day, and enjoy splendid dinners in the evening.

Titanic's Third Class public rooms were not luxurious, but they were pleasantly roomy and comfortable, as here in the smoking room.

Titanic's Third Class passengers on the lower decks included many poor migrants on their way to America. Although they paid the cheapest fares, their lounges and dining rooms were better than on most ships. Third Class families shared cabins with bunk beds, while single men slept in two large dormitories. There were only two bathrooms in Third Class (one for men and one for women), shared between 710 passengers!

FASCINATING FACTS

- The crew ate and slept in the forward part of the ship, traditionally known as the forecastle or fo'c'sle.

- Second Class cabins were much plainer than First Class cabins. They had bunk beds and single beds, a wardrobe and small settee. They also had a wash-basin, which was a luxury on a ship at this time.

- The beds were bolted to the floors to stop them from moving in bad weather and rough seas.

APRIL 13TH 1912

Icebergs!

Titanic's course across the Atlantic Ocean took it into the path of one of the greatest dangers at sea – icebergs.

FASCINATING FACTS

- *Titanic* was steaming across the North Atlantic almost at full speed, at about 21 knots (24 mph or 39 km/h).

- *Titanic's* first ice warning may have come from the *Rappahannock*, though it's not certain what this ship's position was at the time.

The part of an iceberg that lies below the waterline is the biggest part of the iceberg. That's why drifting icebergs are so dangerous to ships.

Data Diary

- At 10.30 pm on April 13th, *Titanic* is heading towards an icefield about 885 km (550 mi.) away.

- At 11.00 pm on April 13th, *Titanic's* wireless machine stops working. Radio operator Jack Phillips spends the night trying to fix the machine.

Every year, huge chunks of ice break off glaciers along the coast of Greenland and drift south as icebergs. In 1912, all ships' captains crossing the North Atlantic were aware of this danger and kept well clear of the iceberg zone. However, in the spring of 1912, the Arctic ice was drifting farther south than usual.

At 10.30 pm on Saturday 13th April, a warning of ice reached *Titanic*'s radio room. The message came from another ship. The sky had been cloudy, with small waves on the water. Now the sea grew calm and the weather cleared. It felt colder. Lookouts shivered as they kept watch on deck, while *Titanic* steamed on towards New York.

Did you know

- Only about one-seventh of an iceberg floats above the water. Most of it lies under the sea.

- Icebergs can drift as much as 19 km (12 mi.) a day.

- In a calm sea, icebergs make no waves and so are hard to see at night.

This newspaper picture of the iceberg that *Titanic* hit was based on sketches made by seaman Joseph Scarrott.

APRIL 14TH 1912

Food and finery

As *Titanic* steamed on through the drifting ice, the ship's 60 chefs and 35 other kitchen staff were busy preparing food. They had over 6,000 meals a day to prepare across six dining rooms and cafés.

The head chef was Charles Proctor, one of the most important and highly paid of the ship's staff. The food prepared was of the highest quality. On the evening of 14th April, many of the First Class passengers sat down to an amazing 10-course dinner. The menu included oysters, poached salmon, chicken Lyonnaise, foie gras, roasted pigeon, lamb with mint sauce and orange ice drenched in champagne.

The tableware from one of *Titanic*'s dining rooms had the flag of the White Star Line in the middle.

The First Class dining saloon on D deck could seat 500 people. Lady Duff-Gordon remembered the daffodils on the tables.

FASCINATING FACTS

⚜ On April 14th, the Café Parisian served a wonderful dinner ending with peaches in Chartreuse jelly and chocolate and vanilla éclairs.

⚜ The expensive Ritz-style restaurant on B Deck was run by chef Gaspare ("Luigi") Gatti, who came from one of London's top restaurants. His staff included a number of his cousins.

Did you know

* Breakfast for some people started with porridge, then kippers or haddock, followed by bacon, sausages, eggs and rolls or toast.

* A typical *Titanic* lunch menu included fish, chicken à la Maryland, mutton chops, a choice of potatoes and vegetables, and a buffet selection including potted shrimps, veal and ham pie and cold meats.

* Sandwiches and cakes were served throughout the day, so passengers never went hungry.

One of *Titanic*'s lunch menus on 14th April offered hot dishes, a cold buffet and a variety of cheeses.

Even Third Class passengers had better food than most ate at home. They had ham and eggs for breakfast, a midday dinner of soup, beef and potatoes and plum pudding, and a supper of cold meat, bread and pickles washed down with plenty of hot tea.

R.M.S. "TITANIC"
APRIL 14. 1912.

LUNCHEON.

CONSOMMÉ FERMIER   COCKIE LEEKIE

FILLETS OF BRILL
EGG À L'ARGENTEUIL
CHICKEN À LA MARYLAND
CORNED BEEF, VEGETABLES, DUMPLINGS

FROM THE GRILL.
GRILLED MUTTON CHOPS
MASHED, FRIED & BAKED JACKET POTATOES

CUSTARD PUDDING
APPLE MERINGUE   PASTRY

BUFFET.
SALMON MAYONNAISE   POTTED SHRIMPS
NORWEGIAN ANCHOVIES   SOUSED HERRINGS
PLAIN & SMOKED SARDINES
ROAST BEEF
ROUND OF SPICED BEEF
VEAL & HAM PIE
VIRGINIA & CUMBERLAND HAM
BOLOGNA SAUSAGE   BRAWN
GALANTINE OF CHICKEN
CORNED OX TONGUE
LETTUCE   BEETROOT   TOMATOES

CHEESE.
CHESHIRE, STILTON, GORGONZOLA, EDAM,
CAMEMBERT, ROQUEFORT, ST. IVEL,
CHEDDAR

Iced draught Munich Lager Beer 3d. & 6d. a Tankard.

Data Diary

* At 5.00 am on April 14th, *Titanic*'s wireless is fixed. The wireless operators have a 6-hour backlog of messages to send.

* At 9.00 am, Captain Smith receives an iceberg warning from RMS *Caronia* reporting "bergs, growlers and field ice".

* At 1.42 pm, another ice warning makes Captain Smith adjust *Titanic*'s course to take the ship farther south.

APRIL 14TH 1912

Don't panic

At 7.30 pm on Sunday 14th, while Captain Smith was at dinner with the First Class passengers, the radio operators received another warning of icebergs, this time from the *Californian*. The captain didn't receive this message.

Just before 9.00 pm, Captain Smith went to the bridge to check all was well. Second Officer Charles Herbert Lightoller was nearing the end of his watch there. At about 9.20 pm Captain Smith went to bed, asking to be woken "if it becomes at all doubtful".

Titanic's First Officer William McMaster Murdoch was on the bridge when *Titanic* struck the iceberg.

Data Diary

⚓ At 9.30 pm, Second Officer Lightoller tells the lookouts to watch out for ice.

⚓ At 9.40 pm, radio operator Jack Phillips receives another ice warning, but sets it aside because he's busy sending and receiving messages for passengers.

⚓ At 10.00 pm, First Officer Murdoch takes over from Lightoller.

⚓ At 10.55 pm, the *Californian* sees ice all around, stops, and warns all ships. Phillips signals back not to bother him, and the *Californian* turns its radio off.

At 11.30 pm *Titanic*'s lookouts saw "a slight haze". At 11.40 pm, they rang the warning bell. There was an iceberg – dead ahead, and only 460 m (1,500 ft) away. First Officer Murdoch told the helmsman to swing the bow to the left, and ordered the engine room to "Stop. Full speed astern". All watertight doors were closed. The ship began to turn away – but it was too late. *Titanic* rammed the iceberg. It was a shock, but there was no need to panic – yet.

Second Officer Lightoller had just gone to bed when he felt the ship hit the iceberg.

Titanic in trouble

When the ship struck the iceberg, many of *Titanic*'s passengers were in bed. At first it seemed nothing was wrong. Then fears began to grow.

The iceberg had ripped open the ship's side. Within 10 minutes, sailors reported 4 m (14 ft) of water flooding the front bow section. Five of *Titanic*'s 16 watertight sections were holed. Water continued to flood in, and the ship began to sink.

In this scene from the 1997 film *Titanic*, water floods the Grand Staircase as the ship takes in more and more water.

John "Jack" Phillips was the senior Marconi wireless operator on board *Titanic*. He had just turned 25 on 11th April, 1912. Jack died in a lifeboat, hours after *Titanic* sank.

Did you know

- *Titanic* sent out distress signals in Morse code, which uses "dots" (short beeps) and "dashes" (long beeps).

- Radio operator Jack Phillips began sending the signal CQD (Come Quick, Danger). This was an emergency code first used in 1904 by Marconi.

- Assistant radio operator Harold Bride said why not try the newer SOS distress signal (dot dot dot, dash dash dash, dot dot dot)? They sent both.

FASCINATING FACTS

- The huge gash in *Titanic*'s side was about 91 m (300 ft) long.

- With their mail room flooding, the postal clerks threw letters into sacks to try and save them.

- Some people asked if the "bump" meant the ship would be late arriving in New York.

Thomas Andrews checked the damage and knew at once that *Titanic* was in trouble. He told Captain Smith the ship would float for perhaps two hours. Help might come from ships nearby, but the captain knew he must get people away in the lifeboats.

Data Diary

- About midnight, Thomas Andrews goes below to inspect the damage.

- By 12.20 am on 15th April, the crew quarters on E Deck are flooded.

- At 12.25 am, *Titanic*'s officers begin helping women and children into the lifeboats.

APRIL 15TH 1912

Into the lifeboats!

At Captain Smith's order, cabin crew hurried to get passengers into the lifeboats. The boats were on the top Boat Deck. They had to be lowered with people inside them.

Officers and stewards went to all First and Second Class cabins, telling passengers to dress quickly in warm clothing. Second Officer Lightoller had pulled on trousers, sweater and coat over his pyjamas. Third Class passengers were left to find their own way to the upper decks. Many were now crowding the corridors, clutching bundles and bags.

No-one yet believed *Titanic* was sinking. How could it? It was the biggest ship in the world. On deck, Fourth Officer Joseph Boxhall saw the lights of a ship. Surely, he thought, it must see the distress rockets he was firing into the night sky? He tried flashing a lamp using Morse code, but to his dismay the ship turned away.

FASCINATING FACTS

- The nearest ship was the *Californian*, about 16 km (10 mi.) away. Fourth Officer Boxhall saw it turn away.

- After the sinking, many people blamed *Californian*'s captain for not coming to help at once.

- *Californian*'s lookouts saw *Titanic*'s distress rockets, but the captain did not go to investigate.

The sea was calm, but as *Titanic* started to list (lean), it took longer to lower the lifeboats and getting them away became harder.

There were enough cork lifejackets for all the passengers and nearly everyone put one on.

Data Diary

🛞 At about 12.35 am, Captain Rostron of the *Carpathia* is told about *Titanic's* distress signal and immediately sets off at full speed (17 knots) for *Titanic's* position, but the ship is 93 km (58 mi.) away, which will take about 4 hours.

🛞 At 12.45 am, *Titanic's* first lifeboat, only half full, is lowered into the water.

APRIL 15TH 1912

SOS!

Several ships picked up *Titanic*'s desperate signals for help. The liner *Carpathia* was now steaming to the rescue, but it was 93 km (58 mi.) away. Would it be in time?

FASCINATING FACTS

- In Lifeboat 8, the Countess of Rothes helped seaman Tommy Jones to steer for hours in the freezing night.

- Molly Brown in Lifeboat 6 helped to row, along with the other women. Later she was nicknamed "Unsinkable Molly Brown".

- One lifeboat had just a single sailor to crew it, so a male passenger who claimed he could sail a yacht was allowed to slide down a rope and join it.

Titanic's two radio operators kept tapping out SOS in Morse code, asking for help and giving the ship's position. All around them confusion was growing. Glasses were moving on tables, chairs starting to slide. The noise of steam blasting from the engine room was so loud that people had to shout to be heard.

The *Carpathia* zigzagged past countless icebergs at full speed, firing rockets every 15 minutes to let *Titanic* know it was coming to the rescue.

Data Diary

☣ At 1.15 am, the water reaches *Titanic*'s name on the ship's bow.

☣ By 1.30 am, *Titanic* is listing (leaning) to starboard (right). *Carpathia* picks up a radio signal from *Titanic* saying "We are sinking fast." On *Carpathia*, every available man is shovelling coal into the furnaces to make the ship go as fast as possible. Blankets are piled in gangways ready for any survivors.

The radio operators stayed at their posts sending out calls for help, until told to leave the ship by Captain Smith.

The first lifeboat to be lowered held only 12 people instead of 48. Among them were Sir Cosmo Duff-Gordon and his wife Lucy. Otherwise the rule was "women and children first". When some men tried to jump into a boat, Second Officer Lightoller waved a gun and told them to get out. Most men stood quietly on deck, watching as the boats rowed away.

Did you know

❧ The lifeboats had rope lifelines along the sides for people in the water to cling on to, but the water was so cold that hardly anyone in the water survived for long.

❧ On board *Carpathia*, the smoking rooms, lounge and library were quickly converted into dormitories ready for any survivors.

APRIL 15TH 1912

Going Down

Nothing could save *Titanic*. As the ship began to sink, people in the lifeboats watched in horror as the ship went down.

At just after 2.00 am, the front of the ship vanished beneath the icy water. Sea water poured in through every opening. Machinery slid forward as the stern rose higher out of the water. The funnels towered above the lifeboats and people clinging to lifebelts in the water. The lights on the ship blazed for a while, then suddenly went dark. The last radio call for help was sent, and the band stopped playing.

Did you know

- The water temperature was below freezing (about -2°C or 28°F).

- The last lifeboat left the ship at 2:05 am, carrying 44 women and children.

- As one of *Titanic*'s funnels crashed down, survivor Richard Williams (the tennis star) saw it kill his father, Charles.

Lifeboats were rowed away to escape being sucked under when *Titanic* sank. A few men found places in the lifeboats, but most were still on the ship. Some lifeboats were only half full.

Newspapers broke the news of the disaster. This headline tells how the ship's band kept playing as the ship sank to help keep the passengers calm.

THE DAILY MIRROR
SATURDAY, APRIL 20, 1912
HYMN PLAYED WHILE THE TITANIC SANK

FASCINATING FACTS

- Survivor Margaret Murphy reported that she saw crew members shutting doors to keep people on the lower decks from escaping.

- Margaret was helped into a lifeboat by two brothers, John and Philip Kiernan.

- The Kiernan brothers were last seen together as *Titanic* went down. They both drowned.

Pulled apart by its own weight, *Titanic* was breaking in two. Hundreds of people were flung into the sea and tried to swim to the lifeboats. Many more were trapped below decks. Most of those in the freezing water died in minutes. By 2.20 am *Titanic* had gone.

Data Diary

- At 2.00 am, 1,500 people are still on board the ship.

- At 2.10 am, Captain Smith tells the two radio officers to save themselves.

- At 2.17 am, Captain Smith is last seen on the bridge.

- At 2.18 am, *Titanic's* lights go out.

- At 2.20 am, the ship sinks.

Rescued

By 2.21 am, all that remained of *Titanic* was a huddle of lifeboats. Many people were in the sea, dead or dying. The living waited to be rescued.

Carpathia raced to the spot at well above its normal speed. It arrived at about 4.00 am. There was no sign of the ship, but then a green flare went up and *Carpathia*'s lookout spotted a lifeboat rising and sinking in the ocean swell. The crew of *Carpathia* started to pick up people from the lifeboats, which were spread over a wide area among the ice floes. The last person to be rescued was Second Officer Lightoller.

Crowds anxiously wait for news of *Titanic* outside the White Star Line's office in the City of London.

Data Diary

- ⚓ At about 8.30 am *Carpathia* picks up the last tired, cold survivors. It has rescued about 710 people (some sources say 705).

- ⚓ At about the same time, the *Californian* arrives – too late to help.

- ⚓ On 15th April, newspaper reports say *Titanic* is being towed to port. Crowds gather at White Star's offices for news.

About 1,500 people had died. Captain Smith was dead. So was Thomas Andrews, last seen in one of the fine rooms he had designed, gazing at a painting. J. J. Astor was seen on deck with an Airedale dog, which he'd released from its kennel. White Star owner J. Bruce Ismay had survived.

Did you know

- Some of the big lifeboats picked up people from the smaller lifeboats. Fortunately, the sea was calm.

- Most people who didn't drown in the ship died quickly of cold in the freezing ocean. Lifejackets kept people afloat, but could not keep them warm.

- Some people died when they jumped into the sea – their lifejackets broke their necks.

One of *Titanic*'s lifeboats, with survivors in lifejackets, is picked up by the steamer *Carpathia*.

FASCINATING FACTS

- *Carpathia* had been heading east for the Adriatic port of Fiume (now Rijeka) in Croatia (part of the Austrian Empire in 1912).

- After landing the *Titanic* survivors in New York, *Carpathia* took on fresh food and stores and then resumed its voyage to Fiume.

Survivors' stories

At first newspapers reported *Titanic* was safe, but then survivors began telling their stories. The world was shocked by the scale of the tragedy.

When *Carpathia* arrived in New York on 18th April, 40,000 people waited to greet the survivors and hear their stories. William Carter, aged 11, told how Mr Astor had taken care of his dog. William's mother had managed to get her son into Lifeboat 14 by arguing that he was not "too old". Stewardess Mary Sloan was told by Thomas Andrews to get into a boat, and was one of 20 women crew to survive. Second Officer Lightoller swam to one of the collapsible boats, then took charge of Lifeboat 12. He was one of many heroes that night.

These *Titanic* relics belonged to the Asplund family from Sweden. The watch shows the time the ship sank – 2.20 am. Of the seven family members, the mother and two children survived.

Did you know

- The youngest *Titanic* survivor was Elizabeth "Millvina" Dean. She was just 9 weeks old. Millvina died aged 97 in 2009.

- Mrs Ida Straus refused to get into a lifeboat because she would not be parted from her husband Isidor. He was offered a place, but gave it to his wife's maid. Ida and Isidor were last seen sitting in deck chairs holding hands.

FASCINATING FACTS

- Five of the six children in First Class survived the sinking of the *Titanic*.

- All 24 children in Second Class survived.

- In Third Class, 52 of the 79 children listed as passengers died.

  (Note: Some sources give slightly different figures.)

The Navratil boys were being taken to America by their father. They escaped in a lifeboat, but their father drowned. The toddlers spoke no English, but were later reunited with their French mother after she saw pictures of them in the newspapers. They were the only children on the *Titanic* to survive without a parent or guardian.

Harold Bride, the radio operator, got severe frostbite from the icy water and had to be helped ashore.

Data Diary

- On 16th April, *Carpathia* sends a list of survivors. The list is posted outside the *New York Times* office.

- On 18th April, *Carpathia* arrives in New York and the survivors go ashore.

APRIL 19TH 1912

What went wrong?

The *Titanic* disaster was front-page news around the world. Some 1,500 people were dead. What could have gone wrong?

Some bodies were recovered and buried on land, but most were lost at sea. J. J. Astor's body was found, but not Captain Smith's. About two-thirds of the victims were identified. "Unknowns" were buried in graves marked by numbers rather than names.

The Res

A diagram from *The Sphere* newspaper of 27th April, 1912, shows how *Titanic* scraped past the iceberg.

In the United States and Britain, experts met to hear evidence and judge what went wrong. The two inquiries agreed that there were three main causes of the tragedy. First, *Titanic* did not have enough lifeboats; second, the ship had been going too fast when ice was a danger; and third, lifeboats were not lowered properly, some were only half-full and they held too few trained seamen.

DIAGRAM II.—Scraping Past the Berg.

FASCINATING FACTS

- About 214 crew members survived.
- *Olympic* was due to leave Southampton on April 24th, 1912, on its scheduled run, but the trip was cancelled because striking crew complained there were too few lifeboats.

Did you know

- No one knows exactly how many people were on *Titanic* because some changed their travel plans at the last minute and some didn't use their real names.

- Estimates suggest that of 175 First Class male passengers only 57 survived; of 168 Second Class male passengers only 14 survived; and of 462 Third Class male passengers only 75 survived.

THE SPHERE

...e Star Giving Evidence before Lord Mersey

Lord Mersey

OF SIR RUFUS ISAACS, THE ATTORNEY-GENERAL, ON TUESDAY—DRAWN BY F. MATANIA

The London inquiry into the disaster hears White Star Line's Joseph Bruce Ismay give evidence. Maps and a model of *Titanic* were used during the investigation.

Data Diary

- On 19th April to 25th May, 1912, a series of hearings about the disaster are held in the United States.

- On 2nd May to 3rd July, 1912, the British hold an inquiry into the disaster.

The lessons

The sinking of the *Titanic* was not the end of the giant ocean liner. Even bigger ships were soon crossing the oceans. *Titanic*'s sinking made sea travel safer, after lessons were learned.

FASCINATING FACTS

- Third Class passengers whose bodies were recovered were buried at sea.

- The bodies of most First and Second Class passengers were buried in the United States or Canada.

- *Californian*'s captain came in for criticism for not going to *Titanic*'s aid sooner. The inquiries said that in future, ships' radio rooms must be manned 24 hours a day, every day.

After the *Titanic* disaster, every passenger ship had to carry radio. At first, ships' radio rooms were often tiny, with barely enough room for equipment and operators.

By the 1930s, passenger liners were almost twice the size of *Titanic*. Everyone had learned that no ship was "unsinkable", so these huge ships had more lifeboats and safety drills. Since 1914, an International Ice Patrol has kept watch for icebergs. There is an international agreement on Safety of Life at Sea (SOLAS) to help ships in trouble, and radar and GPS satellite navigation means ships no longer rely on lookouts. Today, a captain knows the exact position of his or her ship.

A C-130 ice patrol plane of the US Coast Guard flies past a giant iceberg in the North Atlantic.

The cruise ship *Costa Concordia* hit the news in January 2012 when it capsized off the coast of Italy after striking rocks, and 32 people died. Even with every modern navigation and safety aid, accidents at sea still happen.

COSTA CONCORDIA

Titanic found

Titanic's whereabouts remained a mystery until 1985. Then, a robot submarine dived deep into the Atlantic and found the lost ship.

Passengers in lifeboats said they'd seen *Titanic* break in two. No-one was sure this was true. Divers even hoped they might find and raise the ship to the surface. *Titanic*'s fate was revealed in 1985. US underwater explorer Robert Ballard and his team sent down the mini-submarine *Argo,* which found the wreck. In 1986 Ballard dived in the bigger submarine *Alvin*, and sent a robot submarine to film right inside *Titanic*. The mighty ship was seen again, broken in two and lying on the seabed in the cold and dark.

FASCINATING FACTS

- *Titanic*'s bow section was less damaged than the stern.

- Lying on the seabed were thousands of items from the ship, including dinner plates, lamps and furniture. Some of these have been brought to the surface.

- Bacteria are eating away at *Titanic*'s metal hull. By 2100, the wreck may be only heaps of rusted metal.

Titanic's rusting bow section and rails were clearly visible under the water.

This underwater photograph shows Captain Smith's bathroom on the *Titanic*, resting on the ocean floor.

Did you know

- *Titanic* lies 3,810 m (12,500 ft) deep.

- The bow and stern parts broke apart, probably soon after the ship vanished beneath the water.

- *Titanic* is about 21 km (13 mi.) from the position its radio operators sent out.

Data Diary

- On 1st September, 1985, *Titanic*'s wreck is discovered on the seabed.

- In 1986, explorer Robert Ballard visits *Titanic* in a submarine.

- In August 2005, the entire wreck of *Titanic* is mapped for the first time.

This artist's impression shows how the wreck appeared to the 1980s deep-sea explorers.

Titanic remembered

The sinking of *Titanic* shocked and saddened people. Today, the ship's story continues to be told, 100 years after its loss.

There have been many other shipwrecks, but *Titanic* seems special. The ship was so big, so new, and everyone was so proud of it. It seemed "unsinkable" – though no one ever actually claimed it was. Its passengers were a mix of rich and poor, millionaires and migrants, old and young.

FASCINATING FACTS

⚓ A major *Titanic* exhibition opened in Belfast, where the ship was built, in 1912.

⚓ The *Titanic* Museum at Branson, Missouri (USA), is a half-size replica of the ship complete with fake iceberg.

⚓ In April 2012, the cruise liner *Balmoral* passed above the spot where *Titanic* lies, and people dropped wreaths on the water to mark 100 years since the sinking.

In the 1958 film *A Night to Remember*, Kenneth More starred as Second Officer Lightoller.

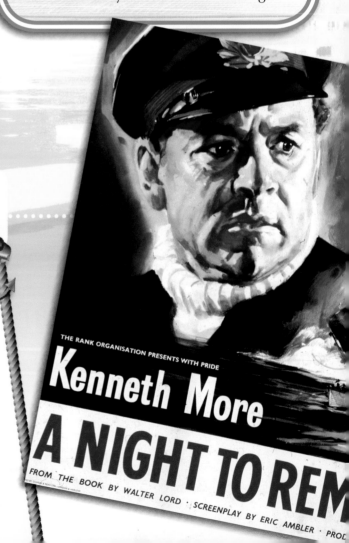

THE RANK ORGANISATION PRESENTS WITH PRIDE

Kenneth More

A NIGHT TO REM

FROM THE BOOK BY WALTER LORD · SCREENPLAY BY ERIC AMBLER · PROD

Data Diary

⚓ In 1997, the film *Titanic* is released. It is directed by James Cameron.

⚓ In 2012, James Cameron, who is also a deep-sea explorer, dives alone in a submersible to the deepest point in the Pacific Ocean – 10,898 m (35,756 ft).

There were stories of great courage, and also stories of people whose courage failed them. No wonder the story has been told so often, by survivors and their families, in newspapers and books, and on radio, TV and the big screen. There are museums and exhibitions devoted to *Titanic*. The ship that lies on the seabed will surely never be forgotten.

In 1914, 100,000 people watched the unveiling of the *Titanic* Engineers Memorial in Southampton. It commemorates the ship's engine-room crew. Many engineers died pumping out water to keep *Titanic* afloat a little longer.

Did you know

- You can find out more about *Titanic* at several UK museums, including the National Maritime Museum in Greenwich, London, and the Merseyside Maritime Museum in Liverpool.

- The many *Titanic* memorials include those at Liverpool, Southampton and Washington, D.C. At Cobh (formerly Queenstown) in Ireland the ship's Irish passengers are remembered.

- Second Officer Charles Herbert Lightoller served in the Royal Navy in World War I. In 1940, during World War 2, he sailed his yacht *Sundowner* to Dunkirk to rescue British soldiers. He died in 1952.

Glossary

bankrupt When a person or company is unable to pay their outstanding debts (money owed).

cabin A room with one or more beds where a passenger sleeps.

cargo Freight or goods carried by a ship.

clipper A fast sailing ship of the 19th century with three or more masts and square sails.

crew People who work on a ship.

cylinder The central working part of a reciprocating engine. Inside the cylinder (a hollow, wide tube) is the piston, which is pushed up and down by steam.

electric bath An early form of tanning bed that used ultraviolet lamps.

hull The main body of a ship. It holds the engines, decks and other fittings.

iceberg A massive chunk of ice that floats in the ocean.

lifeboat A small boat carried on a ship for use in an emergency.

lifejacket A special waistcoat worn to keep people afloat in water.

liner A large, luxurious passenger ship that sailed on a regular route, or line.

migrant Someone who leaves their country to make a new life in another country.

Morse code Signals of dots (short beeps) and dashes (long beeps) used to send messages through wires or the air using wireless (radio).

officer A person on a ship who gives orders. The captain is the most senior officer.

propeller (or screw) A long shaft with two or three blades attached that turn in the water to push (or propel) a ship or boat along.

rivets Metal pegs with round heads, used to fasten a ship's steel plates together.

rudder A flat piece of wood or metal, hinged vertically and mounted at the stern of a ship under the water. The rudder is turned to left or right to change the direction in which the ship is going.

shipyard A place where ships are built, fitted out and repaired.

sidewheel steamer This type of ship had a wooden hull and masts, and engines that turned paddle wheels on the sides of the ship.

slipway A ramp down which a ship slides to enter the water.

turbine An engine with blades turned at high speed by steam.

voyage A long journey made in a ship or boat.

waterline The level reached by the sea on the side of a ship.

wireless A form of radio that in *Titanic's* time used electrical code signals, not voice messages.

INDEX

Index